The Australian Friendship Book

POEMS, QUOTATIONS, GIFTS, AND SHARED MEMORIES

Florence Scott

First published in 1996 by
Gary Allen Pty Ltd
9 Cooper Street
Smithfield NSW Australia

Produced by Sally Milner Publishing Pty Ltd

© in this collection, Gary Allen Pty Ltd

Designed by Griffiths & Young, Canberra
Colour separations and printing by Impact Printing,
Melbourne

Cataloguing in Publication data:
The Australian friendship book: poems, quotations,
gifts and shared memories.

ISBN 1 8751958 X

1. Friendship - Literary collections.
2. Australian literature. I Scott, Florence.

A820.80353

The publishers wish to thank the following
for permission to reproduce work in this collection:
Thea Waddell for Thea Proctor's painting,
'The Rose', featured on the jacket:
Barry Humphries for 'Edna Everage's Favourite
Things' (with apologies to Julie Andrews) and
'A Recipe for Happiness', 1965;
Curtis Brown, Sydney for 'My Country'
by Dorothea Mackellar;
Mushroom Music for '(Give me a)
Home among the gum trees'
by Bob Brown & Wally Johnson;
and Harper Collins Publishers for poems by
Mary Gilmore, David Campbell and
Rosemary Dobson, as well as extracts from
Miles Franklin's 'My Brilliant Career'.

Select some sound hearts.

Be careful not to bruise them with

unfeeling words.

Take of milk of human kindness

one heartful.

Add to this plenty of tact.

Warm the mixture with sympathy.

Do not let it get too hot at first,

lest it only ferment mischief.

Knead with plenty of oil of unselfishness

to make all smooth.

The mixture should be kept in a warm

corner of the heart.

Years only serve to improve the flavour

of friends thus preserved.

BARRY HUMPHRIES · EDNA EVERAGE'S · A RECIPE FOR HAPPINESS

My Country

The love of field and coppice,
Of green and shaded lanes,
Of ordered woods and gardens
Is running in your veins;
Strong love of grey-blue distance.
Brown streams and soft dim skies.
I know but cannot share it,
My love is otherwise.

I love a sunburnt country,
A land of sweeping plains.
Of ragged mountain ranges,
Of droughts and flooding rains;
I love her far horizons
I love her jewel-sea
Her beauty and her terror -
The wide brown land for me!

The tragic ringbarked forests
Stark white beneath the moon,
The sapphire misted mountains.
The hot gold hush of noon.
Green tangle of the brushes
Where lithe lianas coil,
And orchids deck the tree tops
And ferns the crimson soil.

Core of my heart, my country!
Her pitiless blue sky.
When sick at heart around us
We see the cattle die -
But then the grey clouds gather
And we can bless again
The drumming of an army.
The steady soaking rain.

Core of my heart, my country!
Land of the Rainbow Gold,
For flood and fire and famine
She pays us back threefold
Over the thirsty paddocks,
Watch, after many days,
The filmy veil of greenness
That thickens as we gaze.

An opal-hearted country,
A wilful, lavish land -
All you who have not loved her
You will not understand -
Though earth holds many splendours,
Wherever I may die,
I know to what brown country
My homing thoughts will fly.

DOROTHEA MACKELLAR

*I am proud that I am an Australian, a daughter of
the Southern Cross, a child of the mighty bush.
I am thankful I am a peasant, a part of the bone and
muscle of my nation, and earn my bread by the sweat
of my brow, as man was meant to do.*

MILES FRANKLIN - MY BRILLIANT CAREER

*Never allow the thoughtless to declare
That we have no tradition here!*

MARY GILMORE - THE RINGER

*The land I love above all others - not because it was
kind to me, but because I was born on Australian soil,
and because of the foreign father who died at his work
in the ranks of Australian pioneers, and because of
many things. Australia! my country! Her very name is
music to me. God bless Australia! For the sake of the
great hearts of the heart of her!*

HENRY LAWSON - THE ROMANCE OF THE SWAG

Edna Everage's favourite things

White cabbage-moths round tomatoes flitting,
The swish of a sprinkler, the smell of new knitting,
Tea leaves on the maidenhair, silverfish in the bath,
The sugar-ants' trail up my front cement path,
Snails in the letter-box, moths in the lamp,
The design of our latest Australian stamp,
And the Ready Relief that the Raleigh man brings -
These are a few of my favourite things.

BARRY HUMPHRIES FROM THE SHOW 'EXCUSE I'

My books are friends that never fail me.

THOMAS CARLYLE

Friendship is life with understanding.

ANCIENT PROVERB

The best way to cheer yourself up is
to cheer someone else up.

MARK TWAIN

Il faut cultiver notre jardin.

VOLTAIRE

(We must cultivate our garden.)

What I need most of all are flowers, always, always.

CLAUDE MONET

If a man does not make new aquaintances as he advances through life, he will soon find himself left alone. A man, sir, should keep his friendship in constant repair.

SAMUEL JOHNSON

Friendship is always a sweet responsibility, never an opportunity.

KAHLIL GIBRAN

To everything there is a season, and a time for every purpose under the heaven.

ECCLESIASTES 3:1

Buttercups and daisies,
Oh, the pretty flowers;
Coming 'ere the springtime,
To tell of sunny hours.

MARY HOWITT

A rose can say 'I love you',
orchids can enthrall,
but a weed bouquet in a
chubby fist,
oh my, that says it all.

BARBARA JOHNSON

Little drops of water,
Little grains of sand,
Make the mighty ocean,
And the pleasant land.

Little deeds of kindness,
Little words of love,
Make our world an Eden
Like the heaven above.

JULIA A. FLETCHER CARNEY

Pleasant sights and
good reports give
happiness and health.

PROVERBS 15:30

What's in a name? That which we call a rose
By any other name would smell as sweet.

WILLIAM SHAKESPEARE 'ROMEO AND JULIET'

Gather ye rosebuds while ye may
Old time is still a-flying
And that same rose that smiles today
tomorrow will be dying.

ROBERT HERRICK 'TO THE VIRGINS TO MAKE MUCH OF TIME'

Where you tend a rose, my friend,
a thistle cannot grow.

Friends are flowers in the garden of life.

Kind words are like honey - enjoyable and healthful.

PROVERBS 16:24

Rose Hip Jam

truly delicious and a luxury

1 LITRE HIPS

1 LITRE WATER

500 GRAMS OF SUGAR FOR EACH

500 GRAMS OF STRAINED PULP

Boil the hips until they are tender, mashing them with a wooden spoon. Force the pulp through a sieve to remove the seeds. Boil the sugar and the pulp together until a jelly thermometer registers 220°C. Place in sterilised jars and cover.

Rose Water

to keep skin beautiful and soft

Fill a kettle half full of water and add rose petals until the kettle is almost full. Attach tubing to the spout of the kettle and place the kettle over a low heat. The other end of the tubing should be placed in a bottle on the floor. Arrange the tubing so that part of it is submerged in cold water or ice between the spout and the bottle.

As the water boils, the steam will flow through the tubing, carrying with it the aromatic oil from the rose petals. As the vapour passes through the tubing it is cooled by the water or ice and condenses as rose water in the kettle.

Flowers of the Month

January - Delphinium

February - Poppy or Gladiolus

March - Aster

April - Calendula or Gladiolus

May - Chrysanthemum

June - Poinsettia

July - Carnation or Snowdrop

August - Primrose or Violet

September - Daffodil or Jonquil

October - Sweet pea or Daisy

November - Lily-of-the-valley

December - Rose or Honeysuckle

Birthday Flowers
of the Month

AUSTRALIAN NATIVES

January - Flannel flower

February - Native violet

March - Bottlebrush

April - Native fuchsia

May - Tea tree

June - Gum blossom

July - Pea flower

August - Native orchid

September - Boronia

October - Sturt's desert pea

November - Wattle

December - Christmas bells

The kiss of the sun for pardon,
The song of the birds for mirth,
One is nearer God's Heart in a garden
Than anywhere else on earth.

DOROTHY FRANCES GURNEY

Earth laughs in flowers.

RALPH WALDO EMERSON

Love comforteth like sunshine after rain.

WILLIAM SHAKESPEARE

There's a very special garden
Where the flowers of friendship grow...
It's nurtured by the kindness
And concern that good friends show...
The seedlings are the helpful deeds
That friends so gladly do,
And love and laughter are the showers
that strengthen and renew.

AUTHOR UNKNOWN

The perfume of the wind-blown flowers,

The glowing warmth of summer sun,

A little kindness from a friend,

The daily loaf; some work well done.

My slippers when my feet feel tired,

A favourite book, some music gay,

The knowledge that God's arms are near!

These things have brought me joy today.

JOYCE FRANCES CARPENTER

Send a message with flowers

❀ ACACIA - *secret love* ❀ AGRIMONY - *thankfulness, gratitude*

❀ ALMOND, FLOWERING - *hope* ❀ ALOE - *grief, affection*

❀ ALYSSIUM - *worth beyond beauty* ❀ AZALEA - *true to the end* ❀ BLUEBELL - *constancy* ❀ CACTUS - *warmth*

❀ CHRYSANTHEMUM - *love* ❀ CLEMATIS - *mental beauty* ❀ COREOPSIS - *love at first sight* ❀ CROCUS, SAFFRON - *mirth*

❀ DAFFODIL - *regard* ❀ FORGET-ME-NOT - *true love*

❀ HEARTSEASE - *remembrance* ❀ HONEYSUCKLE - *bonds of love* ❀ HYACINTH, BLUE - *constancy* ❀ IVY - *friendship, fidelity*

❀ JASMINE, WHITE - *amiability* ❀ LEMON BLOSSOMS - *fidelity in love* ❀ LILY-OF-THE-VALLEY - *return of happiness* ❀ MAGNOLIA - *dignity* ❀ MARIGOLD - *happiness* ❀ MIMOSA - *sensitivity* ❀ OAK LEAVES - *bravery* ❀ OLIVE - *peace* ❀ ORANGE BLOSSOMS - *purity and loveliness* ❀ PANSY - *loving thoughts* ❀ PEACH BLOSSOM - *captivation* ❀ PEARS -

affection ❀ PEPPERMINT - *warmth of feeling* ❀ PERIWINKLE,

BLUE - *early friendship* ❀ PINK, CARNATION - *woman's love*

❀ PINK, RED, DOUBLE - *pure and ardent*

love ❀ PINK, SINGLE - *pure love* ❀ RANUNCULUS - *charm*

❀ POPPY, SCARLET - *extravagance* ❀ RASPBERRY - *remorse*

❀ ROSE - *love* ❀ ROSE, CABBAGE - *ambassador of love* ❀

ROSE, YELLOW -*decrease of love, jealousy* ❀ ROSE, WHITE

AND RED TOGETHER - *unity* ❀ ROSEMARY - *remembrance*

❀ SNOWDROP - *hope* ❀ SORREL - *affection* ❀ SPEARMINT

- *warmth of sentiment* ❀ STOCK - *lasting beauty* ❀ SWEET

BASIL - *good wishes* ❀ SWEET PEA -*sweet lasting pleasures* ❀

SWEET WILLIAM - *gallantry* ❀ TULIP, RED - *declaration of*

love ❀ VERBENA, SCARLET - *sensibility* ❀ VERBENA,

WHITE - *pure and guileless* ❀ VERONICA - *fidelity* ❀ VIOLET,

BLUE - *faithfulness* ❀ WHITE LILY - *purity and modesty* ❀

WISTARIA - *dependence* ❀ ZINNIA - *thoughts of absent friends*

Like everyone else I feel the need of relations and friendship, of affection, of friendly intercourse, and I cannot miss these things without feeling, as does any other intelligent man, a void and deep need. I tell you this to let you know how much good your visit has done me.

VINCENT VAN GOGH

Friendship is tested in the thick years of success rather than in the thin years of struggle.

BARRY HUMPHRIES

A faithful friend is a strong defence: and he that hath found one hath found a treasure.

ECCLESIASTICUS 6: 14

Friendship is the poetry of life.

ANONYMOUS

A friend should bear his friend's infirmities.

WILLIAM SHAKESPEARE

A friend in need is a friend indeed.

ENGLISH PROVERB

Our affections are our life. We live by them; they supply our warmth.

WILLIAM ELLERY CHANNING

*There was a definite process by which one made
people into friends, and it involved talking to
them and listening to them for hours at a time.*

REBECCA WEST

*Guard within yourself that treasure, kindness.
Know how to give without hesitation,
how to lose without regret, how to acquire
without meanness.
Know how to replace in your heart,
by the happiness of those you love,
the happiness that may be wanting in yourself.*

GEORGE SAND

*The lovely in life is the familiar, and only
the lovelier for continuing strange.*

WALTER DE LA MARE

*Let us not love in word, neither in tongue;
but in deed and truth.*

1 JOHN 3:18

*Write it on your heart that every day
is the best day of the year.*

RALPH WALDO EMERSON

As long as your eyes are blue

Wilt thou love me, sweet, when my hair is grey,
And my cheeks shall have lost their hue?
When the charms of youth shall have passed away,
Will your love as of old prove true?
For the looks may change, and the heart may range,
And the love be no longer fond;
Wilt thou love with truth in the years of youth
And away to the years beyond?

Oh, I love you sweet, for your locks of brown
And the blush on you cheek that lies -
But I love you most for the kindly heart
That I see in your sweet blue eyes -
For the eyes are signs of the soul within,
Of the heart that is real and true,
And mine own sweetheart, I shall love you still,
Just as long as your eyes are blue.

For the locks may bleach, and the cheeks of peach
May bereft of their golden hue;
But mine own sweetheart, I shall love you still,
Just as long as your eyes are blue.

A.B. ('BANJO') PATERSON

*He loved birds and green places and the
wind on the heath, and saw the brightness
of the skirts of god.*

INSCRIPTION ON THE TOMBSTONE OF THE PRESIDENT OF
THE BIRD PROTECTION SOCIETY

Life is nothing without friendship.

CICERO

He who plants a garden plants happiness.

CHINESE PROVERB

*Some people are always grumbling because roses
have thorns. I am thankful that thorns have roses.*

Be slow in choosing a friend, slower in changing.

BENJAMIN FRANKLIN

*A cheerful look brings joy to the heart,
and good news gives health to the bones.*

PROVERBS 15:30

Love forgets mistakes;
nagging about them parts
the best of friends

PROVERBS 17:9

♥

The most I can do for my friend is
simply to be his friend.

HENRY DAVID THOREAU

♥

And the song, from beginning to end,
I found in the heart of a friend.

HENRY WADSWORTH LONGFELLOW

♥

Fragrance always clings to the
hand that gives you a rose.

CHINESE PROVERB

♥

A true friend is always loyal.

PROVERBS 17:17

The Women of the West

They left the vine-wreathed cottage and the mansion on the hill,
The houses in the busy streets where life is never still,
The pleasures of the city, and the friends they cherished best:
For love they faced the wilderness - the Women of the West.

The roar, and rush, and fever of the city died away,
And the old-time joys and faces - they were gone for many a day;
In their place the lurching coach-wheel, or the creaking bullock chains,
O'er the everlasting sameness of the never-ending plains.

In the slab-built, zinc-roofed homestead of some lately-taken run,
In the tent beside the bankment of a railway just begun,
In the huts on new selections, in the camps of man's unrest,
On the frontiers of the Nation, live the Women of the West.

The red sun robs their beauty, and in weariness and pain,
The slow years steal the nameless grace that never comes again;
And there are hours men cannot soothe, and words men cannot say -
The nearest woman's face may be a hundred miles away.

The wide Bush holds the secrets of their longings and desires,
When the white stars in reverence light their holy altar-fires,
And silence, like the touch of god, sinks deep into the breast -
Perchance He hears and understands the Women of the West.

For them no trumpet sounds the call, no poet plies his arts -
They only hear the beating of their gallant, loving hearts,
But they have sung with silent lives the song all songs above -
The holiness of sacrifice, the dignity of love.

Well have we held our father's creed. No call has passed us by.
We faced and fought the wilderness, we sent our sons to die.
And we have hearts to do and dare, and yet, o'er all the rest,
The hearts that made the Nation were the Women of the West.

GEORGE ESSEX EVANS

Time is
Too slow for those who wait,
Too swift for those who fear,
Too long for those who grieve,
Too short for those who rejoice,
But for those who love, time is
Eternity. Hours fly, flowers die,
new days, new ways, pass by.
Love stays.

AUTHOR UNKNOWN

♥

Letter writing is the only device for
combining solitude and good company.

LORD BYRON

♥

A faithful friend is the medicine of life.

ECCLESIASTICUS 6:16

♥

Be not forgetful to entertain strangers: for thereby
some have entertained angels unawares.

HEBREWS 13:2

♥

Life is to be fortified by many friendships. To love
and be loved is the greatest happiness of existence.

SYDNEY SMITH

My grandmother, living to be ninety, met
Whatever chanced with kindness, held her head
On one side like a sparrow, had a bird's
Bright eyes. At dinner used to set
An extra place for strangers. This was done
She said, in Bendigo and Eaglehawk, it was
A custom she observed.

ROSEMARY DOBSON - AMY CAROLINE

♥

Oh, be swift to love! Make haste to be kind.
Do not delay; the golden moments fly!

HENRY WADSWORTH LONGFELLOW

♥

Who can say more than this rich praise,
that you alone are you?

WILLIAM SHAKESPEARE

♥

The love we give away is the only love we keep.

♥

Cheerfulness and contentment are great beautifiers
and are famous preservers of youthful good looks.

CHARLES DICKENS

♥

Happiness is sewing.

Waltzing Matilda

Oh! there once was a swagman camped in a Billabong,
Under the shade of a Coolibah tree;
And he sang as he looked at his old billy boiling,
'Who'll come a-waltzing Matilda with me?'

Who'll come a-waltzing Matilda, my darling,
Who'll come a-waltzing Matilda with me?
Waltzing Matilda and leading a water-bag -
Who'll come a-waltzing Matilda with me?

Down came a jumbuck to drink at the water-hole,
Up jumped the swagman and grabbed him in glee;
And he sang as he stowed him away in his tucker-bag,
'You'll come a-waltzing Matilda with me?'

Down came the Squatter a-riding his thoroughbred;
Down came Policemen - one, two and three.
'Whose is the jumbuck you've got in the tucker-bag?
You'll come a-waltzing Matilda with me?'

But the swagman he up and he jumped in the water-hole,
Drowning himself by the Coolibah tree;
And his ghost may be heard as it sings in the billabong,
'Who'll come a-waltzing Matilda with me?'

A.B. ('BANJO') PATERSON

Life gets better
As I grow older
Not giving a damn
And looking slantwise
At everyone's morning.

ROSEMARY DOBSON - CANBERRA MORNING

If I'd been a housemaid,
I'd have been the best
in Australia - I couldn't help it.
It's got to be perfection for me.

DAME NELLIE MELBA

Grow old along with me!
The best is yet to be.

ROBERT BROWNING

So long as we love we serve; so long as we are loved by
others I would almost say that we are indispensable;
and no man is useless while he has a friend.

ROBERT LOUIS STEVENSON

This was life - my life - my career, my brilliant career!
I was fifteen! A few fleeting hours and I would be old
as those around me. I looked at them as they stood
there, weary, and turning down the other side of the
hill of life. When young, no doubt they had hoped for,
and dreamed of, better things - had even known them.
But here they were.
This had been their life; this was their career.
It was, and in all probability would be, mine too.
My life - my career - my brilliant career!

MILES FRANKLIN - MY BRILLIANT CAREER

You are a part of the universe, no less than the stars
and the trees, and you have a right to be here.
And whether it is clear to you or not, no doubt the
universe is unfolding as it should.

DESIDERATA

Love thy neighbour as much as you love yourself.

MATTHEW 22:39

All who would win joy, must share it;
happiness was born a twin.

LORD BYRON

The thread of our life would be dark,
Heaven knows!
If it were not with friendship
and love intertwin'd.

THOMAS MOORE

Piglet sidled up to Pooh from behind.
'Pooh!' he whispered...'Yes, Piglet?'
'Nothing,' said Piglet, taking Pooh's paw.
'I just wanted to be sure of you!'

A.A. MILNE

Just the knowledge that a good book
is awaiting one at the end of a long
day makes that day happier.

KATHLEEN NORRIS

The one thing I regret is that I will
never have time to read all the good
books I want to read.

FRANCOISE SAGAN

For whoever knows how to return a
kindness he has received must be a
friend above all price.

SOPHOCLES

Of all the things which wisdom
provides to make life entirely
happy, much the greatest is the
possession of friendship.

EPICURUS

T'was on a Saturdee, in Collins street,
An' - quite by accident, o'course - we meet.
Me pal 'e trots 'er up an' does the toff -
'E allus wus a bloke fer showin' off.
'This 'ere's Doreen,' 'e sez. 'This 'ere's the kid.'
I dips me lid.

C.J. DENNIS

Reprove a friend in secret,
but praise him before others.

LEONARDO DA VINCI

If one falls down, his friend can help him up.
But pity the man who falls and has no one to
help him up!

ECCLESIASTES 4:10

Independence? That's middle class
blasphemy. We are all dependent on one
another, every soul of us on earth.

GEORGE BERNARD SHAW

There's time enough for everything
in the Never-Never.

JEANNIE (MRS AENEUS) GUNN - WE OF
THE NEVER-NEVER

Un cuisinier, quand de jine, Me semble un etre divin
Qui, du fond da sa cuisine, gouverne le genre humain.

MARC-ANTOINE DESAUGIERS

(He who cooks food for me, seems like a divine human being who
rules the human race from the depths of the kitchen.)

Fare thee well for I must leave thee,
Do not let this parting grieve thee.
Just remember that the best of
friends must part.

ANONYMOUS

The first duty of love is to listen.

PAUL TILLICH

Happiness arises in the first place
from the enjoyment of one's self,
and, in the next, from the
friendship and conversations of a
few select companions.

JOSEPH ADDISON

Relationships are not
answers to problems.
They are rewards for getting
your life in order.

Mary had a little lamb,
Its fleece was white as snow,
And everywhere that Mary went
That lamb was sure to go.

MRS SARAH JOSEPHA HALE

I have lost friends, some by
death...others through sheer
inability to cross the street.

VIRGINIA WOOLF - THE WAVES

Damper

The Australian damper is a mixture of plain flour with a little salt and enough water to mix. The skill is in the cooking. Alfred Joyce, a Port Phillip District squatter, described how he went about it:

'In the forenoon the flour of the damper was mixed in the iron pot and when thoroughly kneaded the hearth was prepared by carefully setting aside all unburnt wood and embers till nothing remained but the clear, glowing ashes, which were then well opened out, leaving a hollow in the middle for the reception of the dough, the drawn up ridge round it being ready to cover it when placed in its bed, which latter was finally prepared by flattening it down smoothly with the bottom of the frying pan. The damper dough, in the shape of a flat round cake, about two or three inches thick and about fifteen inches across, was then laid carefully in its place and finally covered up with raised ashes around the edges, where it was allowed to remain till a knife inserted in it showed no signs of unbaked dough. It was then taken up and thoroughly dusted with a cloth to remove any adhering ashes and set aside to cool.'

Lamingtons

2 CUPS SELF-RAISING FLOUR

PINCH SALT

3/4 CUP SUGAR

125 GRAMS BUTTER

3 EGGS

VANILLA ESSENCE

2 CUPS DESICCATED COCONUT

Chocolate icing

2 CUPS ICING SUGAR

4 TABLESPOONS COCOA

125 GRAMS BUTTER

1 TEASPOON VANILLA ESSENCE

WARM WATER

Sift the flour and salt. Cream the sugar and butter and add
the eggs and vanilla essence. Beat well and fold in the flour
and salt mixture and the milk. Grease a lamington tin and
bake in a moderate oven, 180°C, for 30-35 minutes.
Cool on a wire rack.
Sift the icing sugar and cocoa together. Melt the butter,
add the essence and beat into the sugar and cocoa mixture.
Beat well and add water until a suitable consistency while
the icing is still moist.

MAKES ABOUT 24

Pavlova

6 EGG WHITES

1 3/4 CUPS CASTER SUGAR

2 TEASPOONS CORNFLOUR

1 TEASPOON VINEGAR

1 TEASPOON VANILLA ESSENCE

1 1/2 CUPS CREAM, WHIPPED

1 TABLESPOON ICING SUGAR

PASSIONFRUIT PULP AND/OR OTHER FRUITS

Beat the egg white until it forms into stiff peaks.
Gradually add caster sugar, beat until thick and
glossy. Fold in flour, vinegar and vanilla essence.

Line an oven tray with baking powder and spread
mixture onto it in a circular or oblong shape,
making the edges slightly raised.

Bake in oven on low heat for about an hour or
until lightly coloured. Cool.

Mix cream and icing sugar together and spread
over the base. Top with fruit.

Seville Orange Marmalade

10 ORANGES

5 LEMONS

4 LITRES WATER

4 KG SUGAR

Wash the fruit and slice finely. Discard the seeds and soak the rest of the fruit in water for 48 hours. Transfer the fruit and water to a large saucepan and bring to the boil. Cook gently until the rind is soft, approximately 30-45 minutes. Add the sugar and cook rapidly, stirring all the time, until the mixture begins to jell, approximately 45-60 minutes. Test to see if it is cooked by placing a small portion on a cold saucer and seeing if it jells.
Pour into warm, sterilised jars and seal.

MAKES APPROXIMATELY 2 LITRES

Fig Jam

1 KG FIGS

90 GRAMS PRESERVED GINGER

3/4 CUP ORANGE JUICE

1/4 CUP LEMON JUICE

2 TABLESPOONS SWEET SHERRY

1 KG SUGAR

Wash the figs and chop roughly. Finely chop the ginger and place the figs and ginger in a saucepan with juices and sherry. Bring to the boil, reduce the heat and cook until the fruit is tender. Add the sugar and stir until dissolved. Boil rapidly, uncovered, until the jam jells when tested on a cold saucer (approximately 25 minutes). Pour into hot sterilised jars and seal.

MAKES APPROXIMATELY 1 LITRE

Star Signs

★ DECEMBER 23 - JANUARY 20 - *Capricorn* Ambitious, persevering, patient, adaptable and reliable. ★ JANUARY 21- FEBRUARY 18 - *Aquarius* Sociable, progressive, democratic, idealistic. ★ FEBRUARY 19 - MARCH 20 - *Pisces* Imaginative, artistic, idealistic. ★ MARCH 21 - APRIL 20 - *Aries* Self-reliant, enthusiastic and courageous. ★ APRIL 21 - MAY 21 - *Taurus* Stable, persevering, aesthetic, sensual, loyal, committed. ★ MAY 22 - JUNE 22 - *Gemini* Stimulating, refreshing, intellectual. ★ JUNE 23 - JULY 23 - *Cancer* Intuitive, sensitive, responsive, nurturing, protective. ★ JULY 24 - AUGUST 23 - *Leo* Successful, able, attractive, generous, noble of spirit, childlike, fun-loving. ★ SEPTEMBER 24 - OCTOBER 23 - *Libra* Engaging, sociable, outgoing, unselfish, objective, impartial. ★ AUGUST 24 - SEPTEMBER 23 - *Virgo* Analytical, logical, perfectionist, useful, exacting, gentle. ★ OCTOBER 24 - NOVEMBER 22 - *Scorpio* Resourceful, probing, analytical, secretive, intense. ★ NOVEMBER 23 - DECEMBER 22 - *Sagittarius* Independent, spirited, energetic, curious.

Birthstones

JANUARY - *Garnet*

FEBRUARY - *Amethyst*

MARCH - *Bloodstone*

APRIL - *Diamond*

MAY - *Emerald*

JUNE - *Pearl*

JULY - *Ruby*

AUGUST - *Sardonyx*

SEPTEMBER - *Sapphire*

OCTOBER - *Opal*

NOVEMBER - *Topaz*

DECEMBER - *Turquoise*

A gift is a precious stone in the
eyes of him that hath it.

PROVERBS 17:8

Pleasant sights and good
reports give happiness
and health.

PROVERBS 15:30

Fame is the scentless sunflower,
with gaudy crown of gold;
But friendship is the breathing
rose, with sweets in every fold.

OLIVER WENDELL HOLMES

When a man is gloomy, everything
seems to go wrong; when he is
cheerful, everything seems right!

PROVERBS 15: 15

A friend is, as it were,
a second self.

CICERO

A good deed is never lost; he
who sows courtesy reaps
friendship, and he who plants
kindness gathers love.

ST BASIL

Talk not of wasted affection;
affection never was wasted.

HENRY WADSWORTH
LONGFELLOW

Life is learning to live,
learning to live and love,
learning to love and lose,
learning to lose and sigh,
learning to sigh and dream,
learning to dream and die.

FRANCIS ADAMS

Unshared joy is an
unlighted candle.

SPANISH PROVERB

Men and boughs break;
Praise life while you
walk and wake;
It is only lent.

DAVID CAMPBELL

Friendship is a sheltering tree.

SAMUEL TAYLOR COLERIDGE

Blessed are they who have the gift of
making friends, for it is one of God's best
gifts. It involves manythings, but above all,
the power of going out of one's self, and
appreciating whatever is noble and loving
in another.

THOMAS HUGHES

Be a friend to yourself
and others will.

SCOTTISH PROVERB

Love conquers all.
VIRGIL

*F*or there is no friend like a sister
In calm or stormy weather;
To cheer one on the tedious way,
To fetch one if one goes astray.
To lift one if one totters down,
To strengthen whilst one stands

CHRISTINA ROSSETTI

*B*lessed are the
quilters for they shall
be called piecemakers.

A loving heart is the
truest wisdom.

CHARLES DICKENS

*A*bove all, love each
other deeply,
because love covers over a
multitude of sins.

1 PETER 4:8

*O*ne word frees us of
all the weight and
pain of life;
That word is love.

SOPHOCLES

*There's no vocabulary
For love within a family,
love that's lived in
But not looked at,
love within the light of which
All else is seen, the love
within which
All other love finds speech.
This love is silent.*

T.S. ELIOT

*Love makes all hard
hearts gentle.*

GEORGE HERBERT

*Strange that I was given
Thoughts that soar to heaven,
Yet must I sit and keep
Children in their sleep!*

DAME MARY GILMORE - THE WOMAN

*A good laugh is
sunshine in a house.*

WILLIAM MAKEPEACE
THACKERAY

*Let me have the
determination to change
what I can change, the
serenity to accept what I
cannot, and the wisdom to
know the difference.*

ST FRANCIS

This house is mine
And yet not mine.
I shall go
Another will come.
Oh god! Who'll
Be the last one?

GERMAN WORDS QUOTED BY SUSAN IRVINE

Happy the man, and happy he alone,
He who can call today his own:
He who, secure within, can say,
Tomorrow, do thy worst,
For I have lived today.

HORACE

The ornaments of a house are the friends who frequent it.

RALPH WALDO EMERSON

Friendship with oneself is all-important because without it
one cannot be friends with anyone else in the world.

ELEANOR ROOSEVELT

Therefore, as we have opportunity,
let us do good to all people...

GALATIANS 6:10

There is no possession more valuable
than a good and faithful friend.

SOCRATES

Though we travel the world over to find the beautiful,
We must carry it with us, or we will find it not.

RALPH WALDO EMERSON

In our life there is a single colour,
as on an artist's palette, which provides the meaning
of life and art. It is the colour of love.

MARC CHAGALL

♥

Friendship consists in forgetting what one gives
and remembering what one receives.

ALEXANDER DUMAS THE YOUNGER

♥

All life is a boomerang. We receive what we give.

SHIRLEY MACLAINE

♥

A merry heart maketh a cheerful countenance.

PROVERB

♥

Above our life we love a steadfast friend.

CHRISTOPHER MARLOWE

♥

To love oneself is the beginning
of a lifelong romance.

OSCAR WILDE

Only a life lived for others is worthwhile.

ALBERT EINSTEIN

♥

*A true friend unbosoms freely, advises justly, assists readily,
adventures boldly, takes all patiently, defends courageously,
and continues a friend unchangeably.*

WILLIAM PENN

♥

*Never criticise or condemn... Go easy on others;
then they will do the same for you.*

LUKE 6:37

♥

*Your own soul is nourished when you are kind;
it is destroyed when you are cruel.*

PROVERBS 11:17

♥

*Friendship improves happiness and abates misery,
by doubling our joy, and dividing our grief.*

JOSEPH ADDISON

♥

*Now the people say I'd never put such horrors into print
If I wasn't too conceited to accept a friendly hint,
And my desired are certain that I'd profit in the end
If I'd always show my copy to a literary friend.*

HENRY LAWSON - MY LITERARY FRIEND

♥

*Of all the things which wisdom provides to
make life entirely happy, much the greatest is
the possession of friendship.*

EPICURUS

When you're a little girl and you look in an aquarium
and you see fish doing this and that,
and snails and so on, you don't criticise and
say they should do something else.
And that's the way in which I was brought up,
and which in fact I see people.

CHRISTINA STEAD

♥

A heart at peace gives life to the body,
but envy rots the bones.

PROVERBS 14:30

♥

I have decided to stick with love.
Hate is too great a burden to bear.

MARTIN LUTHER KING

♥

A true friend is always loyal.

PROVERBS 17:17A

♥

Surely the world we live in is but the world that lives in us.

DAISY BATES

♥

A friend is a present which you give yourself.

ROBERT LOUIS STEVENSON

♥

The best mirror is an old friend.

ENGLISH PROVERB

♥

A constant friend is a thing rare and hard to find.

PLUTARCH

*There have been many friends with simple tables and
modest cellars, about whom it can be said that the soft
extractive note of an aged cork being withdrawn has been
the true sound of a man opening his heart.*

WILLIAM SAMUEL BENWELL

✿

Real love stories never have endings.

RICHARD BACH

✿

*Let us not become weary in doing good,
for at a proper time we will reap a harvest
if we do not give up.*

GALATIANS 6:9

✿

*If you love only those who love you, what good is that?...
If you are friendly only to your friends, how are you
different from anyone else?*

MATTHEW 5:46-7

✿

*The red rose whispers of passion
And the white rose breathes of love
O' the red rose is a falcon
And the white rose is a dove.*

JOHN B. O'REILLY

Anniversaries

FIRST - *paper*   SECOND - *cotton*

THIRD - *leather*

FOURTH - *silk, flowers or books*

FIFTH - *wood*

SIXTH - *iron or sugar*

SEVENTH - *copper or wool*

EIGHT - *bronze*

 NINTH - *pottery*

TENTH - *tin*

ELEVENTH - *steel*

TWELFTH - *linen or silk*

THIRTEENTH - *lace*

FOURTEENTH - *ivory*

FIFTEENTH - *crystal*

THIRTIETH - *pearls*

THIRTY-FIFTH - *coral*

FORTIETH - *ruby*

FORTY-FIFTH - *sapphire*

FIFTIETH - *gold*

 FIFTY-FIFTH - *emerald*

SIXTIETH - *diamond*

SEVENTY-FIFTH - *diamond or platinum*

Hedonist's Chocolate Cake

90 GRAMS DARK CHOCOLATE

125 GRAMS BUTTER

1 1/2 CUPS BROWN SUGAR

1 TEASPOON VANILLA ESSENCE

3 EGGS

1 CUP SOUR CREAM

2 TABLESPOONS COCOA

1/2 CUP HOT WATER

2 1/2 CUPS SELF-RAISING FLOUR

PINCH SALT

Chop chocolate and melt over hot water, put aside until cold. Beat together butter, sugar and vanilla essence until creamy, then beat in the eggs, melted chocolate and sour cream. Mix cocoa into the hot water, sift together flour and salt and stir into creamed mixture, alternately with the cocoa-hot water mixture. Evenly divide between two greased 23 cm sandwich tins and bake in a moderate oven for about 30 minutes. Leave in tins for a few minutes and turn out carefully. Leave to cool thoroughly and join with frosting as well as adding frosting to the tops and sides.

Frosting

60 GRAMS DARK CHOCOLATE

60 GRAMS BUTTER

250 GRAMS ICING SUGAR

2 TABLESPOONS COCOA

1/4 CUP MILK

1 TEASPOON VANILLA ESSENCE

Chop chocolate, put into a small, heavy-based saucepan with butter and stir over low heat until just melted. Sift together icing sugar and cocoa, mix with milk and vanilla essence. put bowl into a larger bowl containing a little ice water and beat with a wooden spoon until thick enough to spread and hold its shape.

Love's done a bunk, an' joy is up the pole;
An' shame an' sorrer's roostin' in me soul.

C.J. DENNIS

❧

If you wait for perfect conditions,
you will never get anything done.

ECCLESIASTES 11:4

❧

Do not worry about tomorrow...
Each day has enough trouble of its own.

MATTHEW 6:34

❧

For the winter is past, the rain is over and gone.
The flowers are springing up and the time of the
singing of the birds has come. Yes, spring is here.

SONG OF SOLOMON 2:11-12

❧

Pursuing an art is not just a matter of
having the time - it is a matter of having a free
spirit to bring to it.

STELLA BOWEN

❧

Mid pleasures and palaces we may roam,
Be it ever so humble, there's no place like home.

J.H. PAYNE

❧

*A friendly discussion is as stimulating as
the sparks that fly when iron strikes iron.*

PROVERBS 27:17

*A thing of beauty is a joy forever;
Its loveliness increases; it will never
pass into nothingness.*

JOHN KEATS

*Vivez, si m'en croyes, n'attendez a demain:
Gueillez des aujourd'hui le roses de la vie.*

(Live, take my advice, don't wait until tomorrow:
Pick the roses of life today.)

*Don't be too eager to tell others their faults,
for we all make many mistakes...*

JAMES 3:1

And now these three remain: faith, hope and love...

1 CORINTHIANS 13:3

*Above all else guard your affections.
For they influence everything else in your life.*

PROVERBS 4:23

There is a time for work and a time for love.
That leaves no other time.

COCO CHANEL.

Old books, old wine, old Nankin blue,
All things, in short, to which belong,
The charm, the grace, that Time makes strong -
All these I prize, but (entre nous)
Old friends are best!

AUSTIN DOBSON

Love is patient, love is kind...
It always protects, always trusts,
always hopes, always perseveres.

1 CORINTHIANS 13:4 AND 7

A cheerful heart is good medicine.

PROVERBS 17: 22A

Always I have a chair for you in the smallest
parlour in the world, to wit, my heart.

EMILY DICKENSON

Clancy of the Overflow

I had written him a letter which I had, for want of better
Knowledge, sent to where I met him down the Lachlan, years ago;
He was shearing when I knew him, so I sent the letter to him,
Just on spec, addressed as follows, 'Clancy of the Overflow.'

And an answer came, directed in a writing unexpected
(And I think the same was written with a thumb-nail dipped in tar):
'Twas a shearing mate who wrote it, and verbatim I will quote it:
"Clancy's gone to Queensland droving, and we don't know
where he are."

In my wild erratic fancy visions come to me of Clancy
Gone a-droving "down the Cooper" where the Western drovers go;
As the stock are slowly stringing, Clancy rides behind them singing,
For the drover's life has pleasures that the townsfolk never know.

And the bush has friends to meet him,
and their kindly voices greet him
In the murmur of the breezes and the river on its bars,
And he sees the vision splendid of the sunlit plains extended,
And at night the wondrous glory of the everlasting stars.

I am sitting in my dingy little office, where a stingy
Ray of sunlight struggles feebly down between the houses tall,
And the foetid air and gritty of the dusty dirty city,
Through the open window floating, spreads its foulness over all.

And in place of lowing cattle, I can hear the fiendish rattle
Of the tramways and the buses making hurry down the street;
And the language uninviting of the gutter children fighting
Comes fitfully and faintly through the ceaseless tramp of feet.

And the hurrying people daunt me, and their pallid faces haunt me
As they shoulder one another in their rush and nervous haste,
With their eager eyes and greedy,
and their stunted forms and weedy,
For townsfolk have no time to grow, they have no time to waste.

And I somehow rather fancy that I'd like to change with Clancy,
Like to take a turn at droving where the seasons come and go,
While he faced the round eternal of the cash-book and the journal -
But I doubt he'd suit the office, Clancy of the Overflow.

A.B. ('BANJO') PATERSON

Do but consider, however, if we live apart,
as we must, it is much the same whether I am
hundreds or thousands of miles distant from you.
The same Providence will watch over us there as here.
The sun that shines on you will also afford me
the benefit of its cheering rays...

ELIZABETH MACARTHUR, TO HER MOTHER.

A companion loves some agreeable
qualities which a man may possess,
but a friend loves the man himself.

JAMES BOSWELL

True happiness consists, not in the multitude
of friends, but in the worth and choice.

BEN JONSON

Friendship is the marriage of the soul.

VOLTAIRE

I would be friends with you and have your love.

WILLIAM SHAKESPEARE

There's a track winding back to an
old-fashioned shack,
Along the road to Gundagai,
Where the blue gums are growing and
the Murrumbidgee's flowing
Beneath that sunny sky.
Where my daddy and mother are waiting for me,
And the pals of my childhood once more I will see,
Then no more will I roam,
when I'm heading right for home
Along the road to Gundagai.

JOHN FRANCIS O'HAGAN

Give me a home among the gum trees,
With lots of plum trees,
A sheep or two and a kangaroo;
Clothesline out the back,
Verandah out the front,
And an old rocking chair...

WALLY JOHNSON AND BOB BROWN

The typical Australian was seldom religious in the sense in which the word is generally used. So far as he held a prevailing creed, it was a romantic one, inherited from the gold-miner and the bushman, of which the chief article was that a man should at all times and at any cost stand by his mate.
That was and is the one law which the good Australian must never break. It is bred in the child and stays with him through life.

C.E.W. BEAN

The only way to have a friend is to be one.

RALPH WALDO EMERSON

Hold a true friend with both your hands

NIGERIAN PROVERB

A friend may be reckoned the masterpiece of nature.

RALPH WALDO EMERSON

A friend is someone you want to be around when you feel like being yourself.

If ever I be worthy or famous -
Which I'm sadly beginning to doubt -
When the angel whose place 'tis to name us
Shall say to my spirit, 'Pass out!'
I wish for no snivelling about me
(My work was the work of the land),
But I hope that my country will shout me
The price of a decent brass band.

HENRY LAWSON - THE JOLLY DEAD MARCH

Above all else guard your affections.
For they influence everything else in your life.

PROVERBS 4:23

I think these difficult times have helped me to
understand better than before how infinitely rich and
beautiful life is in every way and that so many things
that one goes around worrying about are of no
importance whatsoever.

ISAK DINESEN

A friend loves at all times...

PROVERBS 17:17

What is a mate nowadays? Somebody you can rely on - through thick, thin and middling; past hell and high-water. Like the mariner's compass he always points north to you. In any trouble, you know what he will do, without argument; because, since he is your mate, it is exactly what you would do yourself. Your mate is indeed yourself in another fellow's skin - perhaps your better self, perhaps your worse self...

Seems contradictory, doesn't he? - your mate. He is! My Australian oath he is! Look at my mate! Take it from me, there never was such a dogmatic, obstinate, prejudiced, pig-headed son of a twisted mallee root since mates were discovered.
Yet I stick to him; I can't get rid of him - he's inside my skin; he's me, bother him.

THOMAS DODD (QUOTED IN THE AUSTRALIAN WORKER)

Look fer yer profits in the 'earts o' friends,
Fer 'atin' never paid no dividends.

C.J. DENNIS

We sits an' thinks beside the fire,
With all the stars a-shine,
An' no one knows our thoughts but me
An' that there dog o' mine.
We has our Johnny-cake an' scrag,
An' finds 'em fairly good;
He can do anything but talk -
An' wouldn't, if he could.

HENRY LAWSON 'DOWN THE RIVER'

★

It's bad enough to be a bloke
Without one real close friend;
But when your dog gives you the bird
It's pretty near the end.

C.J. DENNIS

*Having someone wonder where you are when you
don't come home at night is a very old human need.*

MARGARET MEAD

*Keep a green bough in your heart and
the singing bird will come.*

CHINESE PROVERB

*Be kindly affectioned one to
another with brotherly love.*

ROMANS

Friendship is love with understanding.

ANCIENT PROVERB

*The greatest happiness of life is the conviction
that we are loved, loved for ourselves, or rather
loved in spite of ourselves.*

VICTOR HUGO

*Under the magnetism of friendship the modest
man becomes bold; the shy confident.*

WILLIAM M. THACKERAY

*Our chief want in life is someone who
will make us do what we can.*

RALPH WALDO EMERSON

The Man from Snowy River

There was movement at the station, for the word had passed around
That the colt from old Regret had got away,
And had joined the wild bush horses -'e was worth a thousand pound,
So all the cracks had gathered to the fray.
All the tried and noted riders from the stations near and far
Had mustered at the homestead overnight,
For the bushmen love hard riding where the wild bush horses are,
And the stock-horse snuffs the battle with delight.

There was Harrison, who made his pile when Pardon won the Cup,
The old man with his hair as white as snow;
But few could ride beside him when his blood was fairly up
He would go wherever horse and man could go.
And Clancy of the Overflow came down to lend a hand,
No better horseman ever held the reins;
For never horse could throw him while the saddle-girths would stand
-he learnt to ride while droving on the plains.

And one was there, a stripling on a small and weedy beast;
He was something like a racehorse undersized,
With a touch of Timor pony - three parts thoroughbred at least -
And such as are by mountain horsemen prized.
He was hard and tough and wiry - just the sort that won't say die -
There was courage in his quick impatient tread;
And he bore the badge of gameness in his bright and fiery eye,
And the proud and lofty carriage of his head.

But still so slight and weedy, one would doubt his power to stay,
And the old man said, 'That horse will never do
For a long and tiring gallop - lad, you'd better stop away,
Those hills are far too rough for such as you.'
So he waited sad and wistful - only Clancy stood his friend -
'I think we ought to let him come,' he said:
'I warrant he'll be with us when he's wanted at the end,
For both his horse and he are mountain bred.

'He hails from Snowy River, up by Kosciusko's side,
Where the hills are twice as steep and twice as rough;
Where a horse's hoofs strike firelight from the flint-stones every stride,
The man that holds his own is good enough.
And the Snowy River riders on the mountains make their home,
Where the river runs those giant hills between;
I have seen full many horsemen since I first commenced to roam,
But nowhere yet such horsemen have I seen.'

So he went; they found the horses by the big mimosa clump,
They raced away towards the mountain's brow,
And the old man gave his orders, 'Boys, go at them from the jump,
No use to try for fancy riding now.
And, Clancy, you must wheel them, try and wheel them to the right.
Ride boldly, lad and never fear the spills,
For never yet was rider that could keep the mob in sight,
If once they gain the shelter of those hills.'

So Clancy rode to wheel them - he was racing on the wing
Where the best and boldest riders take their place,
And he raced his stock-horse past them, and he made the ranges ring

With the stockwhip, as he met them face to face.
Then they halted for a moment, while he swung the dreaded lash,
But they saw their well-loved mountain full in view,
And they charged beneath the stockwhip with
a sharp and sudden dash,

And off into the mountain scrub they flew.
Then fast the horsemen followed, where the gorges deep and black
Resounded to the thunder of their tread,
And the stockwhips woke the echoes, and they fiercely answered back
From cliffs and crags that beetled overhead.
And upward, ever upward, the wild horses held their way,
Where mountain ash and kurrajong grew wide;
And the old man muttered fiercely, 'We may bid the mob good day,
No man can hold them down the other side.'

When they reached the mountains summit, even Clancy took a pull -
It well might make the boldest hold their breath;
The wild hop scrub grew thickly, and the hidden ground was full
Of wombat holes, and any slip was death.
But the man from Snowy River let the pony have his head,
And he swung his stockwhip round and gave a cheer,
And he raced him down the mountain like a torrent down its bed,
While the others stood and watched in very fear.

He sent the flint-stones flying, but the pony kept his feet,
He cleared the fallen timber in his stride,
And the man from Snowy River never shifted in his seat -
It was grand to see that mountain horseman ride.
Through the stringybarks and saplings,
on the rough and broken ground,

Down the hillside at a racing pace he went;
And he never drew the bridle till he landed safe and sound
At the bottom of that terrible descent.

He was right among the horses as they climbed the farther hill,
And the watchers on the mountain, standing mute,
Saw him ply the stockwhip fiercely; he was right among them still,
As he raced across the clearing in pursuit.
Then they lost him for a moment, where two mountain gullies met
In the ranges - but a final glimpse reveals
On a dim and distant hill side the wild horses racing yet,
With the man from Snowy River at their heels.

And he ran them single-handed till their sides were white with foam;
He followed like a bloodhound on their track,
Till they halted, cowed and beaten; then he turned their heads for home,
And alone and unassisted brought them back.
But his hardy mountain pony he could scarcely raise a trot,
He was blood from hip to shoulder from the spur;
But his pluck was still undaunted, and his courage fiery hot,
For never yet was mountain horse a cur.

And down by Kosciusko, where the pine-clad ridges raise
Their torn and ragged battlements on high,
Where the air is clear as crystal, and the white stars fairly blaze
At midnight in the cold and frosty sky,
And where around The Overflow the reed-beds sweep and sway
To the breezes, and the rolling plains are wide,
The Man from Snowy River is a household word today,
And the stockmen tell the story of his ride.

A. B. 'BANJO' PATERSON

Pot pourris

to scent your rooms and bring back memories

Australian bush pot pourri

2 CUPS DRIED GUM LEAVES

1 CUP ANY DRIED LEMON-SCENTED BUSH LEAVES

(LEMON-SCENTED EUCALYPTS, BOTTLEBRUSH,
TEA-TREE OR MYRTLE)

1 CUP WATTLE FLOWERS

8 WHOLE CRUSHED CLOVES

6 DROPS EUCALYPTUS OIL

A FEW INTERESTING SEED PODS, OR WHOLE DRIED
OR PRESSED NATIVE FLOWERS FOR DECORATION.

Place the dry mix and the fixative into your container
and gently shake or mix well. With an eye dropper, add the
fragrant oil one drop at a time, mixing well between drops.
Cover the pot pourri and put it aside for a few days in
a cool, dark place. Shake or stir now and then to allow
the fragrances to blend.
If the scent is not strong enough add some more oil,
one drop at a time. Mix well between drops. Take care not to
add too much oil, or the scent will be overpowering.
Put the pot pourri mix into decorative jars and pots when
you are satisfied with the perfume.

Rose pot pourri

✿ 3 CUPS OF DRIED ROSE PETALS ✿ 10 DRIED AND
CRUMBLED MINT LEAVES ✿ 10 CRUSHED CLOVES ✿
1/2 TEASPOON GROUND ALLSPICE ✿ 1/2-1 CUP OF
OAKMOSS ✿ 10 DROPS FRAGRANT ROSE OIL

Mix as for bush pot pourri

Rose and lavender pot pourri

✿ 3 CUPS DRIED ROSE PETALS ✿ 1 CUP DRIED LAVENDER ✿
2/3 CUP OF DRIED LEMON VERBENA LEAVES ✿ 1/4 CUP
DRIED MARJORAM ✿ 1/4 CUP DRIED ROSEMARY ✿ 1/2 TO
1 CUP DRIED ORANGE PEEL ✿ 2 TABLESPOONS ALLSPICE ✿
1 TABLESPOON CRUSHED CLOVES ✿ 8 DROPS FRAGRANT
ROSE OIL ✿ 2 DROPS LAVENDER OIL

Mix as for bush pot pourri

Lavender pot pourri

✿ 3 CUPS DRIED LAVENDER FLOWERS ✿ 1 CUP DRIED RED
ROSE PETALS AND ✿ ANY DRIED BLUE OR PURPLE
FLOWERS (FOR COLOUR) ✿ 4 TABLESPOONS DRIED MINT
LEAVES ✿ 2 TABLESPOONS DRIED ROSEMARY ✿ 1 CUP OF
OAKMOSS, OR 1 TABLESPOON OF ORRIS ROOT POWDER ✿
10 DROPS OF FRAGRANT LAVENDER OIL

Mix as for bush pot pourri

*It has always been held for a special
principle in friendship that prosperity provideth
but adversity proveth friends.*

ELIZABETH I TO MARY QUEEN OF SCOTS

*Beauty is but composure, and we find
Content is but the concord of the mind,
Friendship the unison of well-trained hearts
Honour the chorus of the noblest parts.*

KATHERINE FOWLER PHILIPS

Friendship's a noble name, 'tis love refined.

SUSANNAH CENTLIVRE

*Friendship in affectionate bosoms, generally revives
with redoubled tenderness, after a little interruption.*

JANE WEST

Talk not of love, it gives me pain,
For love has been my foe;
He bound me with an iron charm,
And plunged me deep in woe.
But friendship's pure and lasting joys,
My heart was formed to prove.

AGNES CRAIG

Business, you know, may bring money,
but friendship hardly ever does.

JANE AUSTEN

Save thy toiling, spare thy treasure:
All I ask is friendship's pleasure;
Let the shining ore lie darkling,
Bring no gem in lustre sparkling:
Gifts and gold are naught to me,
I would only look on thee.

MARIA BROOKS

Sachets

to scent your drawers and cupboards

A simple sachet made from two
pretty handkerchiefs
and decorated with ribbons and scraps of lace.
Sew the handkerchiefs together on three sides and
fill the bag loosely with your favourite pot pourri.
Close the third side.
Place large sachets among clothing
or use them as a sleep pillow.
A smaller sachet can be made from one
handkerchief and folded in half and sewn on
two sides, filled with pot pourri and tied with a
ribbon. To hang from coathangers or to tuck
among linen.

Herbal bath sachets

Make up a sachet as before but instead of using a
pot pourri mixture, use 1/2 a cup of either dried
lemon verbena, rosemary, lavender or mint or a
mixture of two or three of these.

Pressed flowers

Collect all your favourites together and preserve
for use on cards or simply as mementoes.

Place one or two sheets of absorbent paper into
a wooden press or between the pages of a book.
Place your leaves and flowers into position,
making sure that they do not touch each other
Close and either screw the press down or place
a weight on the book.

Leave for between two and six weeks.

It is wonderful to come across pressed flowers
you have forgotten in a book. And it is
wonderful to add them to a book you are
giving as a gift.

Treat your friends as you do your pictures; place them in their best light.

JENNIE JEROME CHURCHILL

Keep a green bough in your heart and the singing bird will come.

CHINESE PROVERB

You give but little when you give of your possessions. It is when you give of yourself that you truly give.

KAHLIL GIBRAN

I know of only one duty and that is love.

ALBERT CAMUS

When I get a little money, I buy books; and if any is left, I buy food and clothes.

ERASMUS

Friendship is unnecessary, like philosophy, like art... It has no survival value; rather it is one of those things that give value to survival.

C.S. LEWIS

'He was my cobber' - an expressive blend
Of 'mate' and 'pal', more definite than 'brother'
And somewhat less perfunctory than 'friend'.

IFORD, 'THE ARBITER', BULLETIN

One of the best mates I ever
had was a woman, but I didn't
know it till we parted.

BULLETIN

It was not a perfect year.

But has there ever been a perfect year?

Has there ever been a year

When all the love and health and fame

We wished for one another

Ever came to pass?

Yet, despite the disappointments

of these, our complex lives,

We learn to make do - make better - make believe

That better days will come.

And if we continue to believe,

Who is to say that

The perfect year

Will not yet be here?

Advance Australia Fair

Australians all let us rejoice,
For we are young and free;
We've golden soil and wealth for toil;
Our home is girt by sea;
Our land abounds in nature's gifts
Of beauty rich and rare;
In history's page, let every stage
Advance Australia Fair.
In joyful strains then let us sing
Advance Australia Fair.

Beneath our radiant Southern Cross
We'll toil with hearts and hands;
To make this Commonwealth of ours
Renowned of all the lands;
For those who've come across the seas
We've boundless plains to share
With courage let us all combine
To Advance Australia Fair.
In joyful strains then let us sing,
Advance Australia Fair.

PETER DODDS MCCORMICK